Dandelion Readers

Reading and Spelling Activities
The Extended Phonic Code
Level 1

Phonic Books Ltd
www.phonicbooks.co.uk

Introduction

Children learning to read with Synthetic Phonics learn to identify the letters (or groups of letters) in the English Phonic Code and the sounds they represent. They learn to blend the sounds together into words. This is called 'decoding'.   They learn to spell by segmenting a word into its phonemes and using the correct spelling for these phonemes. This is called 'encoding'. The English Phonic Code is a complex code and learning to decode and encode takes a great deal of practice.

The worksheets in this pack offer a number of activities and games to develop these skills. They accompany the books in the Dandelion Readers series – The Extended Phonic Code – Level 1.

In Level 2, two or three spellings are taught for each vowel sound e.g. Book 1 'Viv Wails' introduces the spellings <ai> <ay> <a> for the phoneme 'ae'.

Level 2 complements any phonic programme that is teaching alternative spellings for a sound. The books can also be used as a Special Needs resource for older children who are learning the phonic code at a faster pace.

For an accelerated pace the teacher may choose to teach the additional spellings for that sound e.g. <a-e> and <ea> which are introduced in Level 3 books.

The books and the activities can be used in any order. The teacher can use them while following the structure of any phonic programme being taught.

The Reading and Spelling activities include blending, segmenting and comprehension. Because children learn best when they enjoy themselves, two games have been included in each chapter.

Dandelion Readers
Extended Phonic Code Series

Level 1

	Phoneme	Grapheme	Book
Book 1	ae	ai	The Mail
Book 2	ee	ee	The Tree
Book 3	oe	oa	Raj Gets a Soak
Book 4	er	ur	My Turn
Book 5	e	ea	Bread and Jam
Book 6	ow	ow	Mr Brown
Book 7	b'oo't	oo	Zoom!
Book 8	ie	igh	The Night Flight
Book 9	l'oo'k	oo	In the Wood
Book 10	or	or	The Fort

Level 2

	Phoneme	Grapheme	Book
Book 1	ae	ai, ay, a,	Viv Wails
Book 2	ee	ee, e, ea	Sweet Dreams
Book 3	oe	oa, o, ow	Toad Moans and Groans
Book 4	er	ur, er, ir	Meg Gets Dirty
Book 5	e	ea, e, ai	Raj Bumps his Head
Book 6	ow	ow, ou	The Tree House
Book 7	b'oo't	oo, ew, ue	The Blue Scooter
Book 8	ie	igh, i, y	I Spy
Book 9	l'oo'k	oo, oul, u	The Bush
Book 10	or	or, a, aw	Dan Draws a Monster

Level 3

	Phoneme	Grapheme	Book
Book 1	ae	ai, ay, a, a-e, ea	Jake the Snake
Book 2	ee	ee, e, ea, y	A Heap of Sand
Book 3	oe	oa, o, ow, oe, o-e	Toad in a Hole
Book 4	er	ur, er, ir, or.ear	Pasta with Butter
Book 5	e	<ea> as 'ae' 'e' or 'ee'	The Heavy Robot
Book 6	ow	<ow> as 'ow' or 'oe'	Miss Flower's Project
Book 7	b'oo't	oo, ew, ue, u-e	School Rules
Book 8	ie	igh, i, y, ie, i-e	The Kite
Book 9	l'oo'k	<oo> as 'boot' or 'look'	The Tooth
Book 10	or	or, a, aw, au, al	The Tent on the Lawn

Dandelion Readers

This folder belongs
to

____

www.phonicbooks.co.uk - enquiries@phonicbooks.co.uk – tel:0771963355
Dandelion Readers © 2008 This sheet may be photocopied by the purchaser.

The Extended Phonic Code
Level 1 Book 1

'The Mail' - ‹ai›

Page 1 - Word Building and Blending

Page 2 - Segmenting and Spelling
Words: rain, mail, train, snail, tail

Page 3 - Reading Practice - words with ‹ai›

Page 4 – Reading and Comprehension 1 – Make a Book

Page 5 – Reading Comprehension 2 – What's Missing?

Page 6 - Reading Game

Page 7 – 4-in-a-row Game

Each sheet has it's own instructions.

Level 1 Book 1   'The Mail'   <ai>

Word Building and Blending <ai>

r		n	
n		l	
t	r		n	
s	n		l	

| ai | ai | ai | ai |

Cut out the <ai> squares and slot into the words above.
Blend the sounds into a word. Draw a matching picture of the word in the big box.
This sheet may be photocopied by the purchaser. © Phonics Book Ltd. 2008

Level 1 Book 1   'The Mail'   <ai>

Segmenting and Spelling - words with <ai>

Level 1 Book 1 'The Mail' <ai>

Reading Practice - words with <ai>

pain	wait	tail
nail	sail	maid
bait	paint	main
snail	brain	trail
raid	wail	saint
train	stain	rain
pail	laid	<ai> words

Name: Date: page 4

Level 1 Book 1   'The Mail'   <ai>

Reading and Comprehension 1 – Make a Book

Pip has mail in his bag. Pip has to get the mail to his pals.

Then it begins to rain. Pip cannot get the mail to his pals.

Pip gets nails and a sail. Pip sails on the logs with the mail.

Level 1 Book 1 'The Mail' <ai>

Reading and Comprehension 2 – What's Missing?

Pip has a disco party with his pals.

But then it begins to rain. Pip gets the sail

and the nails. He sets up a tent. The sail

keeps the rain off the bugs. Pip has fun

with his pals.

What's missing in the picture?

Reading Game

Start

Finish

sail		tail	snail	hail		grail
main		fail		grain		faint
pail		rail	paint			aid
rain		pain	aim			jail
snail	mail	train	claim	plain		laid

Play with counters and die. This sheet may be photocopied by the purchaser. © Phonic Books Ltd 2008

4 in a row game <ai>

tail	rain	nail	bait	snail
stain	pail	hail	laid	waist
grain	maid	trail	wail	rail
train	frail	brain	mail	gain
aim	faint	tail	wait	sail
claim	main	rail	train	snail
raid	paint	jail	pain	rain

Play with two sets of coloured counters. Two players take turns to read the word and put a counter on the word. Players can make 4 -in-a row horizontally, vertically and diagonally. The winner is the first to get 4 of his/her counters in a row. The winner places a counter on a dandelion. The game is played four times until all the dandelions are covered. This sheet may be photocopied by the purchaser. © Phonic Books Ltd. 2008

The Extended Phonic Code
Level 1 Book 2

'The Tree' - ‹ee›

Page 1 - Word Building and Blending

Page 2 - Segmenting and Spelling
Words: bee, tree, seed, feet, queen

Page 3 - Reading Practice - words with ‹ee›

Page 4 – Reading and Comprehension 1 – Make a Book

Page 5 – Reading Comprehension 2 – What's Missing?

Page 6 - Reading Game

Page 7 – 4-in-a-row Game

Each sheet has it's own instructions.

Level 1 Book 2   'The Tree'   <ee>

Word Building and Blending <ee>

| b | |

| t | r | |

| s | | d |

| qu | | n |

| ee | ee | ee | ee |

Cut out the <ee> squares and slot into the words above. Blend the sounds into a word. Draw a matching picture of the word in the big box. This sheet may be photocopied by the purchaser. © Phonics Book Ltd. 2008

Level 1 Book 2   'The Tree'   <ee>

Segmenting and Spelling - words with <ee>

Level 1 Book 2   'The Tree'   <ee>

Reading Practice - words with <ee>

feel	weep	see
creep	need	meet
keep	peel	eel
sleep	deep	queen
been	feed	feet
heel	steep	bee
seen	tree	<ee> words

Level 1 Book 2   'The Tree'   <ee>

Reading and Comprehension 1 – Make a Book

Pip and Tess feel hot.
"Get off me bee!"
says Pip to the bee.

Pip and Tess plant a
seed in a deep pit.
Tess keeps it wet.

The seed grows into a
big tree. The tree is
green.

Read the text and draw a picture to match the text on each page. Cut around the boxes and fold into a book.
This sheet may be photocopied by the purchaser. © Phonic Books Ltd. 2008

Level 1 Book 2   'The Tree'   <ee>

Reading and Comprehension 2 – What's Missing?

Tess and Pip have a picnic next to the green tree.   Tess gets green apples and sweets from the bag.   But the greedy bees land on the sweets.   Tess and Pip run off.

What's missing in the picture?

Level 1 Book 2 'The Tree' <ee>

Reading Game

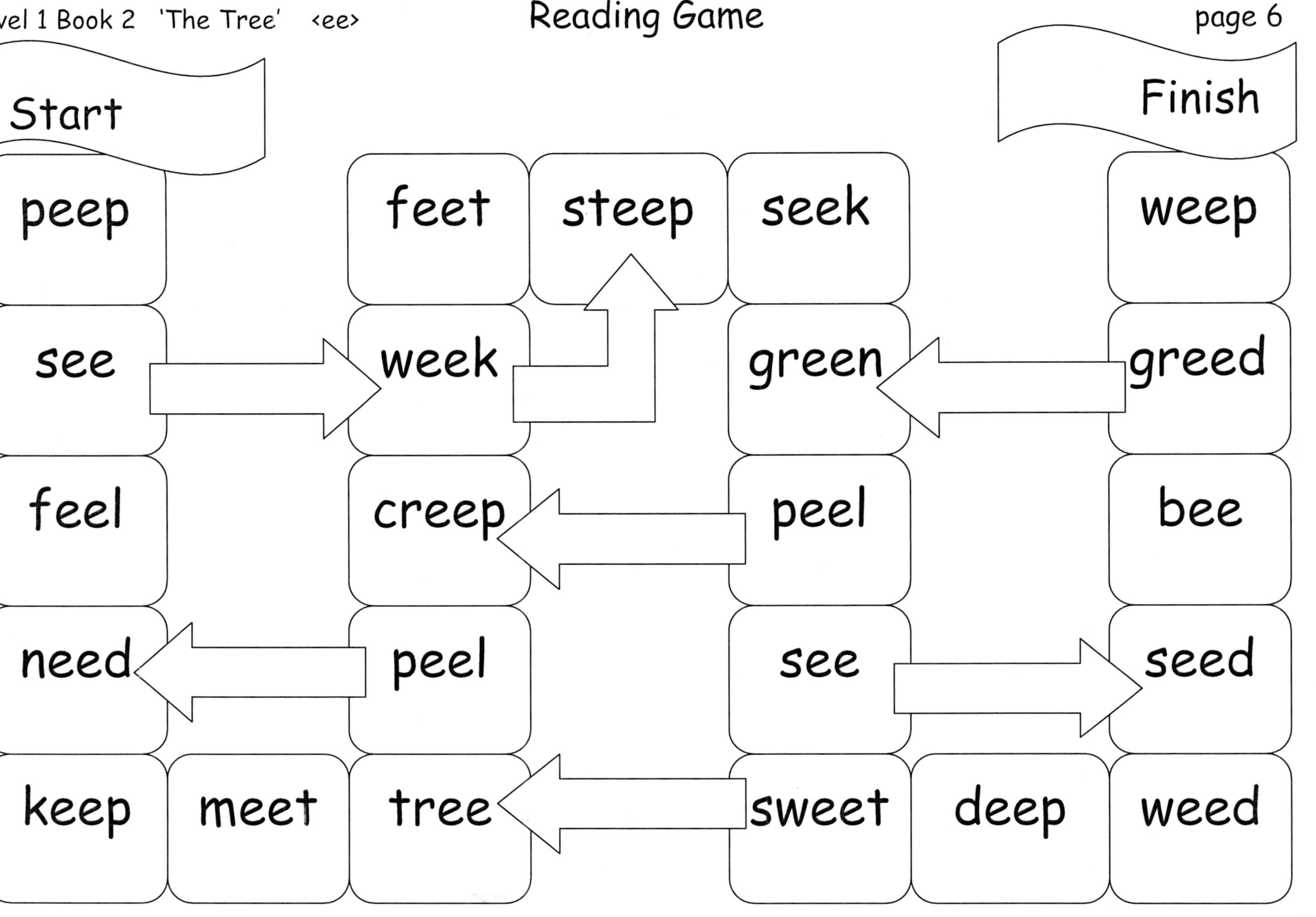

Play with counters and die. This sheet may be photocopied by the purchaser. © Phonic Books Ltd 2008

4 in a row game <ee>

tree	creep	need	breed	sleep
steep	bee	heel	feel	wheel
green	seen	meet	week	feet
keep	peel	greed	deep	sweet
peek	see	speed	need	sleep
weed	creep	peel	green	free
meet	greed	seed	weep	keen

Play with two sets of coloured counters. Two players take turns to read the word and put a counter on the word. Players can make 4 -in-a row horizontally, vertically and diagonally. The winner is the first to get 4 of his/her counters in a row. The winner places a counter on a dandelion. The game is played four times until all the dandelions are covered. This sheet may be photocopied by the purchaser. © Phonic Books Ltd. 2008

The Extended Phonic Code
Level 1 Book 3

'Raj Gets a Soak' - ‹oa›

Page 1 - Word Building and Blending

Page 2 - Segmenting and Spelling
Words: boat, goal, loaf, road, goat

Page 3 - Reading Practice - words with ‹oa›

Page 4 – Reading and Comprehension 1 - Make a Book

Page 5 – Reading Comprehension 2 – What's missing?

Page 6 - Reading Game

Page 7 – 4-in-a-row Game

Each sheet has it's own instructions.

Level 1 Book 3   'Raj Gets a Soak'   <oa>

Word Building and Blending <oa>

b		t	
g		l	
l		f	
s		p	

| oa | oa | oa | oa |

Cut out the <oa> squares and slot into the words above. Blend the sounds into a word. Draw a matching picture of the word in the big box. This sheet may be photocopied by the purchaser. © Phonics Book Ltd. 2008

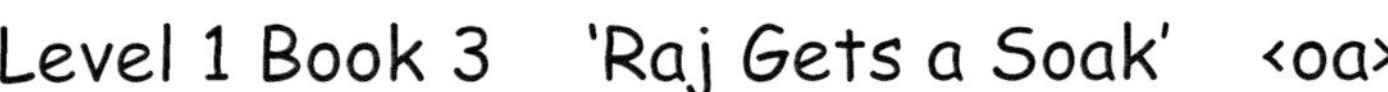

Level 1 Book 3   'Raj Gets a Soak'   <oa>

Segmenting and Spelling - words with <oa>

Write the word for each picture. Put one sound in each square.
This sheet may be photocopied by the purchaser. © Phonic Books Ltd. 2008

Level 1 Book 3   'Raj Gets a Soak'   <oa>

Reading Practice - words with <oa>

boat	road	foal
cloak	soap	moan
loaf	moat	roam
soak	oats	croak
toad	coat	groan
foam	goal	goat
oak	coal	<oa> words

Level 1 Book 3   'Raj Gets a Soak'   <oa>

Reading and Comprehension 1 – Make a Book

Raj is in goal. He grabs the ball. No goal! But Raj lands in the mud.

When Raj gets back he gets into the tub with foam. His Mum rubs his coat.

The next day Raj is back in goal. Raj grabs the ball but he lands in the mud!

Read the text and draw a picture to match the text on each page. Cut around the boxes and fold into a book.

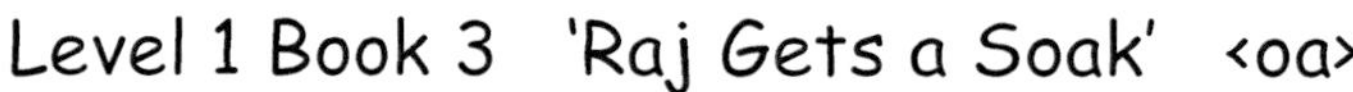

Level 1 Book 3   'Raj Gets a Soak'   <oa>

Reading and Comprehension 2 – What's Missing?

When Raj gets back his Mum groans.

"Look at your coat! I have just scrubbed it

with soap!" she groans. The next day Raj

cannot be in goal. He has to play cricket

with his Dad.

What's missing in the picture?

This text follows on from the story 'Raj Gets a Soak'. The pupil reads the text and adds the missing details in the
picture below. The pupil can then write his or her own ending to the story.
This sheet may be photocopied by the purchaser. © Phonic Books Ltd. 2008

Reading Game

Play with counters and die. This sheet may be photocopied by the purchaser. © Phonic Books Ltd 2008

4 in a row game <oa>

toad	road	moat	boat	soak
load	soap	oats	foal	roam
groan	moan	loaf	foam	goal
goal	oak	boats	coat	load
foal	moan	groan	croak	soap
road	goal	toad	loaf	cloak
soak	oats	boat	moan	groan

Play with two sets of coloured counters. Two players take turns to read the word and put a counter on the word. Players can make 4 -in-a row horizontally, vertically and diagonally. The winner is the first to get 4 of his/her counters in a row. The winner places a counter on a dandelion. The game is played four times until all the dandelions are covered. This sheet may be photocopied by the purchaser. © Phonic Books Ltd. 2008

The Extended Phonic Code
Level 1 Book 4

'My Turn' - <ur>

Page 1 - Word Building and Blending

Page 2 - Segmenting and Spelling
Words: church, fur, curl, surf, hurt

Page 3 - Reading Practice - words with <ur>

Page 4 – Reading and Comprehension 1 – Make a Book

Page 5 – Reading Comprehension 2 – What's Missing?

Page 6 - Reading Game

Page 7 – 4-in-a-row Game

Each sheet has it's own instructions.

Level 1 Book 4   'My Turn'   <ur>

Word Building and Blending <ur>

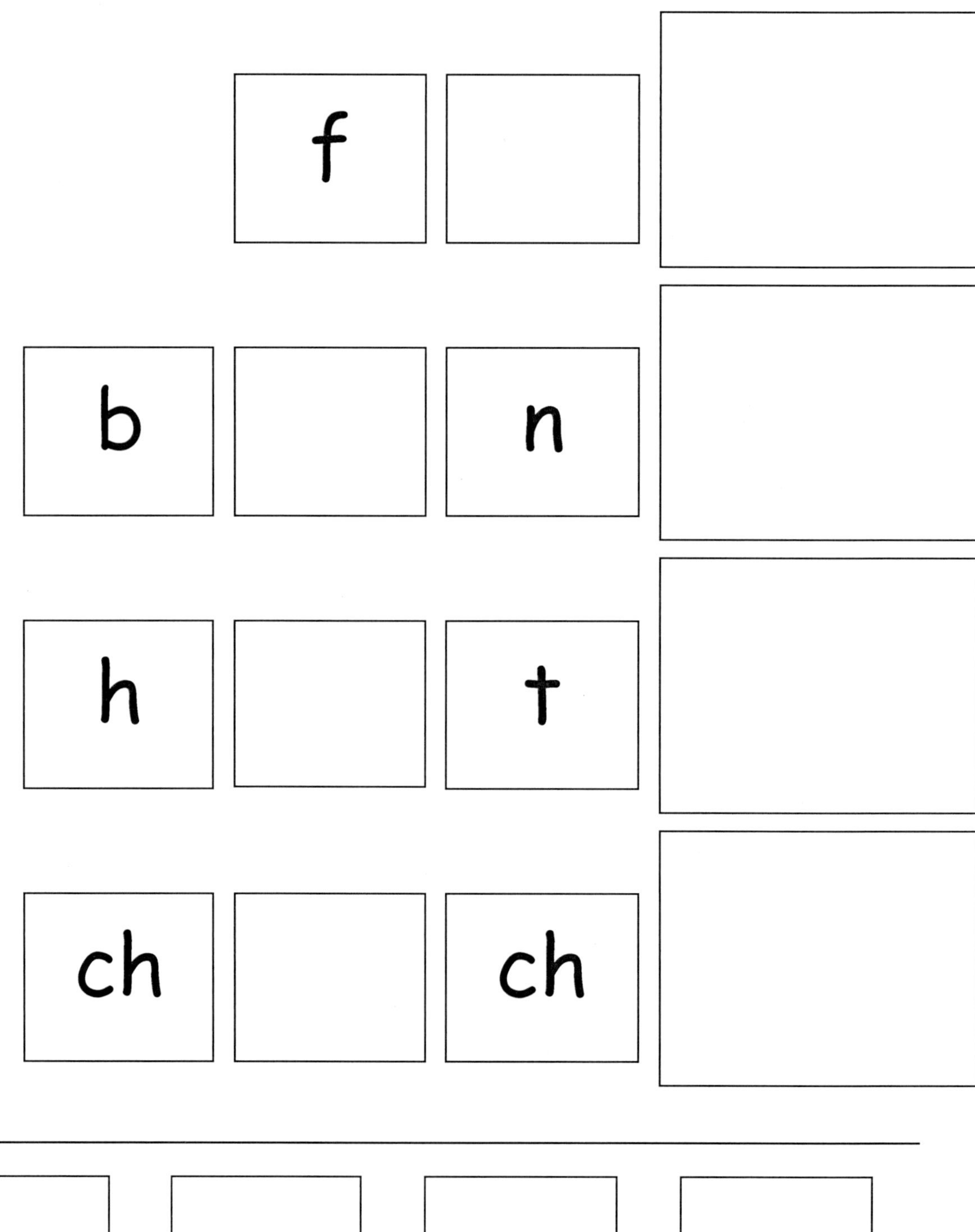

Cut out the <ur> squares and slot into the words above. Blend the sounds into a word.
Draw a matching picture of the word in the big box.
This sheet may be photocopied by the purchaser. © Phonics Book Ltd. 2008

Level 1 Book 4   'My Turn'   <ur>

Segmenting and Spelling - words with <ur>

Write the word for each picture. Put one sound in each square.

Level 1 Book 4   'My Turn'   <ur>

Reading Practice - words with <ur>

Burt	curl	hurt
urn	slurp	turn
burp	lurk	fur
hurl	burst	burn
turns	curls	hurts
hurts	burnt	hurls
curly	surfing	<ur> words

Level 1 Book 4   'My Turn'   <ur>

Reading and Comprehension 1 – Make a Book

Burt is on the hopper. "Can I have a turn?" asks Frank. Burt will not give Frank a turn.

Then Burt is hurled off the hopper. His leg hurts. His hand hurts.

"Burt! You are hurt!" says Frank. He helps Burt up. Frank is a good pal to Burt.

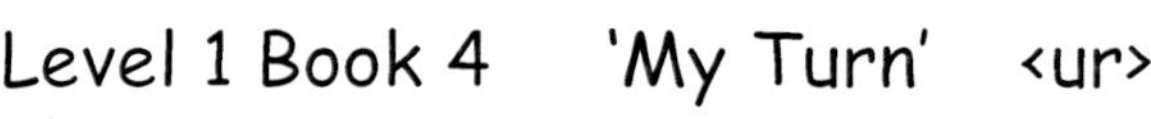

Level 1 Book 4   'My Turn'   <ur>

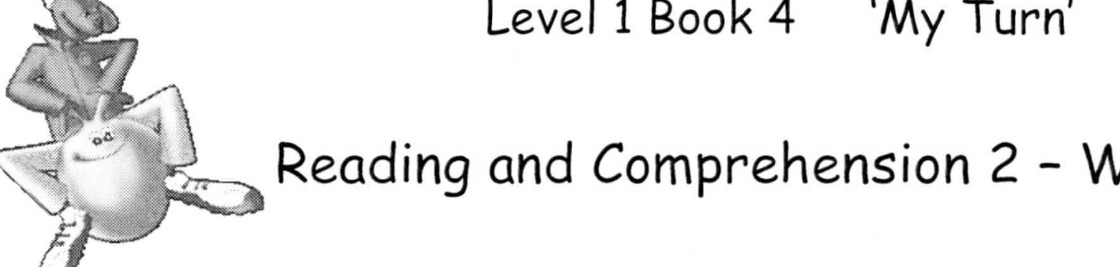

Reading and Comprehension 2 – What's Missing?

When Burt is hurled off the hopper he hurts his hand and his leg. Frank's Mum is a nurse. She checks Burt's hand and leg. "This will help," she says and hands the rabbits cans of pop.

"Slurp," says Burt. "Burp," says Frank.

What's missing in the picture?

Reading Game

Start

turn		Burt	burn	hurl		church
hurt	→	burst		curb	←	burst
curl		surf	←	church		fur
fur	←	turns		lurk	→	urn
burp	urn	lurk	←	hurt	curl	slurp

Finish

4 in a row game <ur>

turn	curl	lurk	burn	church
lurch	surf	Burt	hurt	slurp
hurl	curls	fur	urn	burst
hurts	burns	burp	turn	lurk
fur	surf	burst	hurl	slurp
burb	curl	burnt	urn	church
Burt	hurl	burn	turn	surf

Play with two sets of coloured counters. Two players take turns to read the word and put a counter on the word. Players can make 4 -in-a row horizontally, vertically and diagonally. The winner is the first to get 4 of his/her counters in a row. The winner places a counter on a dandelion. The game is played four times until all the dandelions are covered. This sheet may be photocopied by the purchaser. © Phonic Books Ltd. 2008

The Extended Phonic Code
Level 1 Book 5

'Bread and Jam' - ‹ea›

Page 1 - Word Building and Blending

Page 2 - Segmenting and Spelling
Words: head, bread, feather, sweat, tread

Page 3 - Reading Practice - words with ‹ea›

Page 4 – Reading and Comprehension 1 – Make a Book

Page 5 – Reading Comprehension 2 – What's Missing?

Page 6 - Reading Game

Page 7 – 4-in-a-row Game

Each sheet has it's own instructions.

Level 1 Book 5   'Bread and Jam'   <ea>

Word Building and Blending <ea>

h		d	
t	r		d	
s	w		t	
b	r		d	

---

ea	ea	ea	ea

Cut out the <ea> squares and slot into the words above. Blend the sounds into a word. Draw a matching picture of the word in the big box.

Level 1 Book 5   'Bread and Jam'   <ea>

Segmenting and Spelling - words with <ea>

			er

Write the word for each picture. Put one sound in each square.
This sheet may be photocopied by the purchaser. © Phonic Books Ltd. 2008

Level 1 Book 5   'Bread and Jam'   <ea>

Reading Practice - words with <ea>

head	read	dead
meant	deaf	spread
dreamt	sweat	ready
steady	heads	breakfast
instead	dealt	weapon
heavy	feather	weather
leather	meadow	<ea> words

Level 1 Book 5   'Bread and Jam'   <ea>

Reading and Comprehension 1 – Make a Book

Pip and Tess cut a bit of bread and spread jam on it.
"Don't tread in the jam," says Tess.

But Pip jumps into the jam and lands on his head. Pip has his head stuck in the jam! Help!

Tess pulls Pip off the jam. Pip has jam spread all over his head. He licks the jam on his head. Yum!

Level 1 Book 5   'Bread and Jam'   <ea>

Reading and Comprehension 2 – What's Missing?

"This is my breakfast," said Pip as he licked the jam off his head. But the jam stuck to his head. When Pip got back he ran a hot bath. Then leapt into the bath and scrubbed the jam off his head.

What's missing in the picture?

This text follows on from the story 'Bread and Jam'. The pupil reads the text and adds the missing details in the picture below. The pupil can then write his or her own ending to the story.
This sheet may be photocopied by the purchaser. © Phonic Books Ltd. 2008

Reading Game

Start

Finish

head

dread   heavy   bread

meant

bread   heads   ready   deaf

dealt   dreamt   sweat   heavy

leapt   deaf   leapt   read

meant   sweat   read   spread   dread   dead

4 in a row game <ea>

head	dead	bread	dealt	read
meant	leapt	sweat	spread	heads
dread	bread	head	read	deaf
ready	heavy	steady	sweat	meant
deaf	leapt	bread	dealt	ready
head	health	wealth	sweat	dead
bread	read	heavy	spread	dread

Play with two sets of coloured counters. Two players take turns to read the word and put a counter on the word. Players can make 4 -in-a row horizontally, vertically and diagonally. The winner is the first to get 4 of his/her counters in a row. The winner places a counter on a dandelion. The game is played four times until all the dandelions are covered. This sheet may be photocopied by the purchaser.   © Phonic Books Ltd. 2008

The Extended Phonic Code
Level 1 Book 6

'Mr Brown' - <ow>

Page 1 - Word Building and Blending

Page 2 - Segmenting and Spelling
Words: cow, owl, crown, clown, town

Page 3 - Reading Practice - words with <ow>

Page 4 – Reading and Comprehension 1 – Make a Book

Page 5 – Reading Comprehension 2 – What's Missing?

Page 6 - Reading Game

Page 7 – 4-in-a-row Game

Each sheet has it's own instructions.

Level 1 Book 6   'Mr Brown'   <ow>

Word Building and Blending <ow>

c		
	l	

b	r		n	
c	l		n	

---

ow	ow	ow	ow

Cut out the <ow> squares and slot into the words above. Blend the sounds into a word.
Draw a matching picture of the word in the big box.
This sheet may be photocopied by the purchaser. © Phonics Book Ltd. 2008

Level 1 Book 6   'Mr Brown'   <ow>

Segmenting and Spelling - words with <ow>

Write the word for each picture. Put one sound in each square.

Level 1 Book 6   'Mr Brown'   <ow>

Reading Practice - words with <ow>

cow	owl	how
howl	now	row
gown	brown	town
frown	clown	crowd
flower	power	towel
vowel	vow	scowl
allow	drown	<ow> words

Level 1 Book 6   'Mr Brown'   <ow>

Reading and Comprehension 1 – Make a Book

Mr Brown is the postman. But Meg the dog growls at him. "Growl, growl," says Meg.

Mr Brown mops his brow. "Now how shall I get the post in the post box?" asks Mr Brown.

Mr Brown bends down and hands Meg the post. Now Meg is a post dog! Meg can help Mr Brown.

Read the text and draw a picture to match the text on each page. Cut around the boxes and fold into a book.
This sheet may be photocopied by the purchaser. © Phonic Books Ltd. 2008

Level 1 Book 6   'Mr Brown'   <ow>

Reading and Comprehension 2 – What's Missing?

Meg goes up and down the town with the post. But one day a big cat sits on the path. Meg scowls. The cat says, "Meeow!" Meg growls.   The cat runs. Meg drops the post and runs after the cat.

What's missing in the picture?

This text follows on from the story 'Mr Brown'. The pupil reads the text and adds the missing details in the picture below. The pupil can then write his or her own ending to the story.
This sheet may be photocopied by the purchaser. © Phonic Books Ltd. 2008

Reading Game

Start

cow	owl	flower	towel	owl
now	scowl		vow	down
gown	growl		row	now
howl	drown		crowd	power
town	crown	down	drown	howl	brown

Finish

4 in a row game <ow>

owl	gown	howl	flower	now
how	brown	frown	growl	cow
crown	town	towel	down	clown
drown	owl	crowd	now	how
scowl	crowd	flower	bow	owl
towel	power	allow	vow	clown
row	gown	down	crowd	growl

Play with two sets of coloured counters. Two players take turns to read the word and put a counter on the word. Players can make 4 -in-a row horizontally, vertically and diagonally. The winner is the first to get 4 of his/her counters in a row. The winner places a counter on a dandelion. The game is played four times until all the dandelions are covered. This sheet may be photocopied by the purchaser. © Phonic Books Ltd. 2008

The Extended Phonic Code
Level 1 Book 7

'Zoom' - <oo>

Page 1 - Word Building and Blending

Page 2 - Segmenting and Spelling
Words: boot, roof, moon, roots, spoon

Page 3 - Reading Practice - words with <oo>

Page 4 – Reading and Comprehension 1 – Make a Book

Page 5 – Reading Comprehension 2 – What's Missing?

Page 6 - Reading Game

Page 7 – 4-in-a-row Game

Each sheet has it's own instructions.

Level 1 Book 7   'Zoom'   <oo>

Word Building and Blending <oo>

b		t	
m		n	
r		f	

| s | p | | n | |

| oo | oo | oo | oo |

Cut out the <oo> squares and slot into the words above. Blend the sounds into a word. Draw
a matching picture of the word in the big box.

Level 1 Book 7   'Zoom'

Segmenting and Spelling - words with <oo>

Write the word for each picture. Put one sound in each square.
This sheet may be photocopied by the purchaser. © Phonic Books Ltd. 2008

Level 1 Book 7   'Zoom'   <oo>

Reading Practice - words with <oo>

zoo	cool	soon
boot	hoot	room
tool	pool	loop
fool	droop	stoop
drool	roof	loose
proof	moose	igloo
food	mood	<oo> as in 'boot' words

Level 1 Book 7   'Zoom'   <oo>

Reading and Comprehension 1 – Make a Book

Nan is in a bad mood.
The room is mess!
Nan and Cat get on
the mop and zoom
off.

Nan and cat zoom
onto the roof. Then
they zoom up to the
moon.

Nan and cat land on
the moon. Soon it is
noon.   They have
food on the moon. It
is so cool!

Read the text and draw a picture to match the text on each page. Cut around the boxes and fold into a book.
This sheet may be photocopied by the purchaser. © Phonic Books Ltd. 2008

Level 1 Book 7   'Zoom'   <oo>

Reading and Comprehension 2 – What's Missing?

Nan and cat sit on the moon and have a bit of food. "I must get back," says Nan and she zooms back on the mop. Oops! Oh, no! Nan left cat on the moon. Cat is in a bad mood!

What's missing in the picture?

This text follows on from the story 'Zoom'. The pupil reads the text and adds the missing details in the picture below. The pupil can then write his or her own ending to the story.
This sheet may be photocopied by the purchaser. © Phonic Books Ltd. 2008

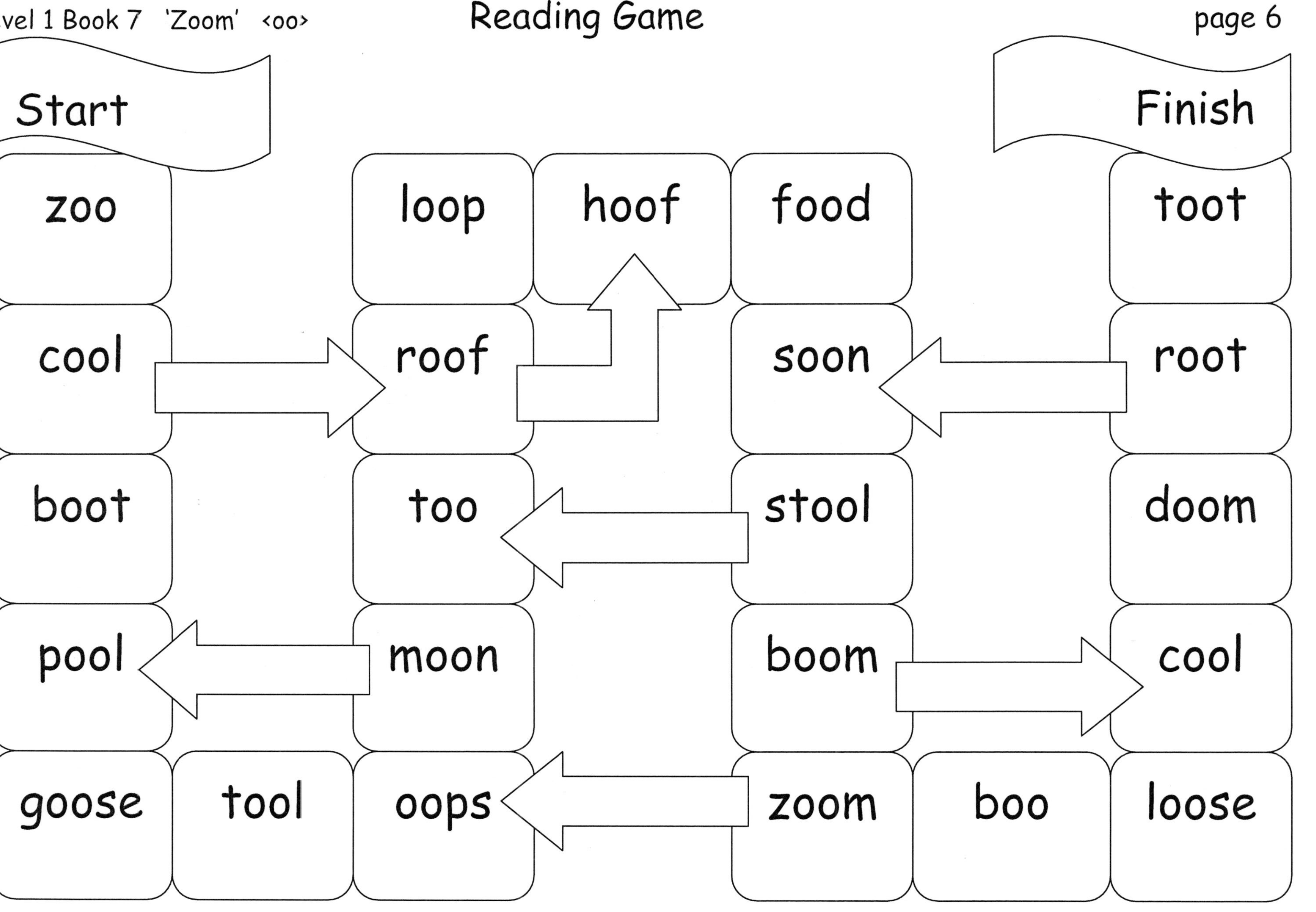

Play with counters and die. This sheet may be photocopied by the purchaser. © Phonic Books Ltd 2008

4 in a row game <oo> as in 'boot'

zoo	tool	too	soon	boo
cool	food	hoof	mood	stool
fool	igloo	oops	cool	boot
moon	root	soon	boom	hoot
toot	stool	bloom	noon	pool
zoom	room	loop	too	roof
moose	boot	goose	hoof	soon

Play with two sets of coloured counters. Two players take turns to read the word and put a counter on the word. Players can make 4 -in-a row horizontally, vertically and diagonally. The winner is the first to get 4 of his/her counters in a row. The winner places a counter on a dandelion. The game is played four times until all the dandelions are covered. This sheet may be photocopied by the purchaser. © Phonic Books Ltd. 2008

The Extended Phonic Code
Level 1 Book 8

'The Night Flight' - <igh>

Page 1 - Word Building and Blending

Page 2 - Segmenting and Spelling
Words: night, light, right, high, flight

Page 3 - Reading Practice - words with <igh>

Page 4 – Reading and Comprehension 1 – Make a Book

Page 5 – Reading Comprehension 2 – What's Missing?

Page 6 - Reading Game

Page 7 – 4-in-a-row Game

Each sheet has it's own instructions.

Level 1 Book 8   'The Night Flight   <igh>

Word Building and Blending <igh>

l		t	
n		t	
f	l		t
b	r		t

| igh | igh | igh | igh |

Cut out the <igh> squares and slot into the words above. Blend the sounds into a word.
Draw a matching picture of the word in the big box.
This sheet may be photocopied by the purchaser. © Phonics Book Ltd. 2008

Level 1 Book 8   'The Night Flight'   <igh>

Segmenting and Spelling - words with <igh>

Write the word for each picture. Put one sound in each square.

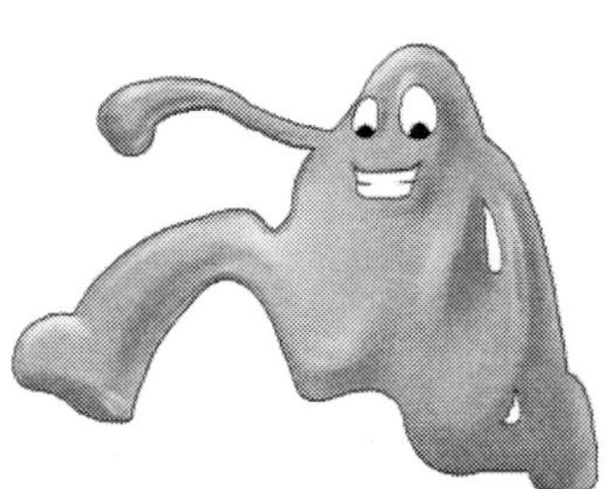

Level 1 Book 8   'The Night Flight'   <igh>

Reading Practice - words with <igh>

high	sigh	tight
right	light	bright
thigh	fright	might
fight	slight	knight
night	sunlight	tonight
midnight	upright	<igh> words

Level 1 Book 8   'The Night Flight'   <igh>

Reading and Comprehension 1 – Make a Book

In the night Zig and
Zog have fun.
"Let's get on the jet
tonight," says Zig.

Zig and Zog hold
tight onto the jet.
They see a bright red
planet on the right.

Zig and Zog meet
Spud on the bright
red planet. Spud gets
on the jet with them.

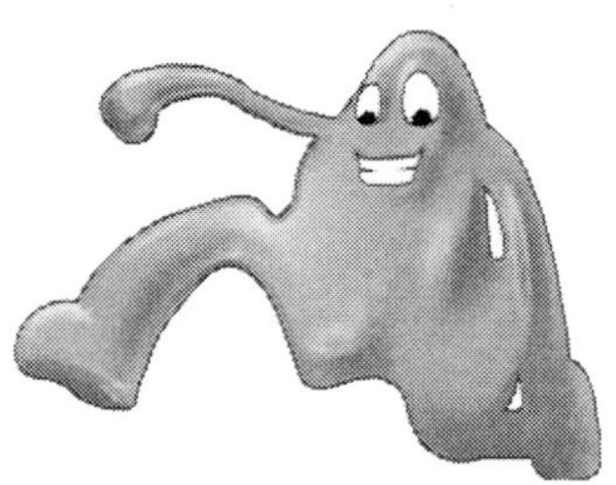

Level 1 Book 8   'The Night Flight'   <igh>

Reading and Comprehension 2 – What's Missing?

Zig, Zog and Spud land on Liz's bed in the night. When it is daylight Liz gets up. She gets a fright when she sees Spud right next to her. But then Spud sighs and gives Liz a tight hug.   "You can be my Mum," he sighs.

What's missing in the picture?

This text follows on from the story 'The Night Flight'. The pupil reads the text and adds the missing details in the picture below. The pupil can then write his or her own ending to the story.
This sheet may be photocopied by the purchaser. © Phonic Books Ltd. 2008

Level 1 Book 8   'The Night Flight' <igh>   Reading Game

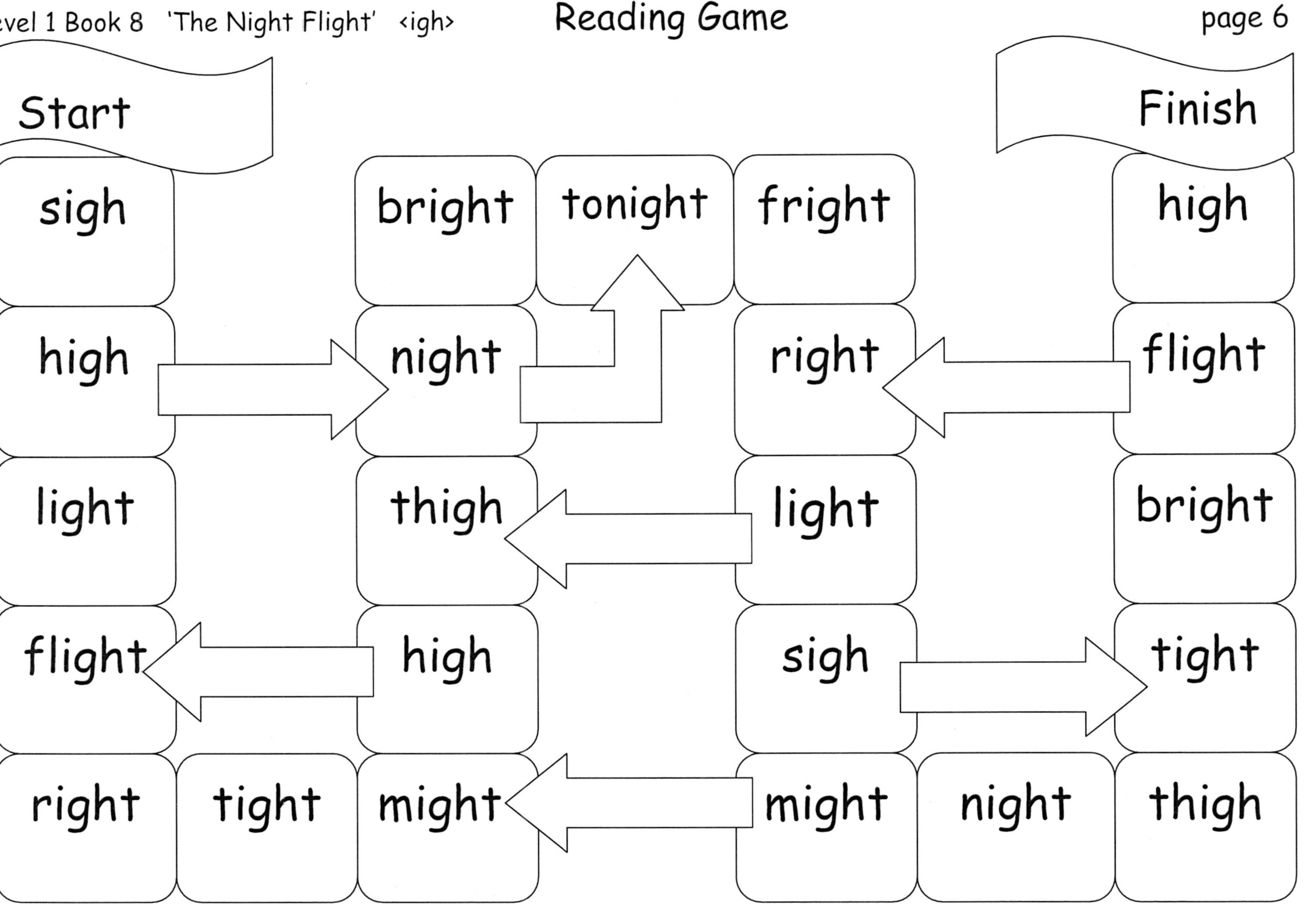

Play with counters and die. This sheet may be photocopied by the purchaser. © Phonic Books Ltd 2008

4 in a row game <igh>

high	night	right	flight	sigh
tight	bright	might	thigh	light
sigh	night	right	tight	fright
flight	bright	might	sight	high
night	light	slight	tight	sigh
might	flight	right	sight	right
light	bright	flight	high	fright

Play with two sets of coloured counters. Two players take turns to read the word and put a counter on the word. Players can make 4 -in-a row horizontally, vertically and diagonally. The winner is the first to get 4 of his/her counters in a row. The winner places a counter on a dandelion. The game is played four times until all the dandelions are covered. This sheet may be photocopied by the purchaser. © Phonic Books Ltd. 2008

The Extended Phonic Code
Level 1 Book 9

'In the Wood' - <oo>

Page 1 - Word Building and Blending

Page 2 - Segmenting and Spelling
Words: book, wood, foot, cook, hood

Page 3 - Reading Practice - words with <oo> as in b'oo'k

Page 4 – Reading and Comprehension 1 – Make a Book

Page 5 – Reading Comprehension 2 – What's Missing?

Page 6 - Reading Game

Page 7 – 4-in-a-row Game

Each sheet has it's own instructions.

Level 1 Book 9   'In the Wood'   <oo>

Word Building and Blending <oo> as in 'book'

b		k	
w		d	
f		t	
c		k	

oo	oo	oo	oo

Cut out the <oo> squares and slot into the words below. Blend the sounds into a word.
Draw a matching picture of the word in the big box.

Name: Date:

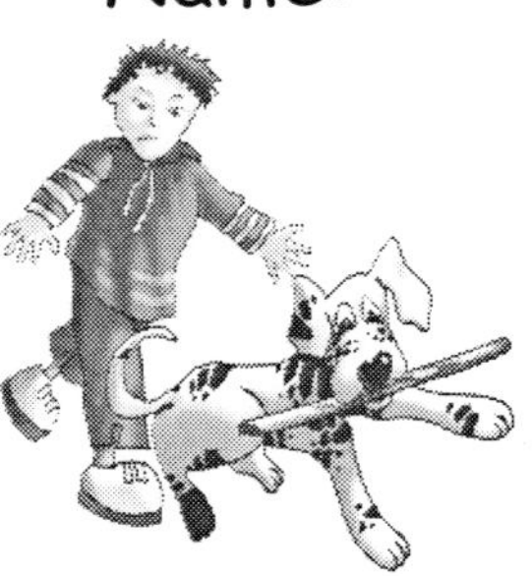

Level 1 Book 9 'In the Wood' <oo>

Segmenting and Spelling – words with <oo> as in 'book'

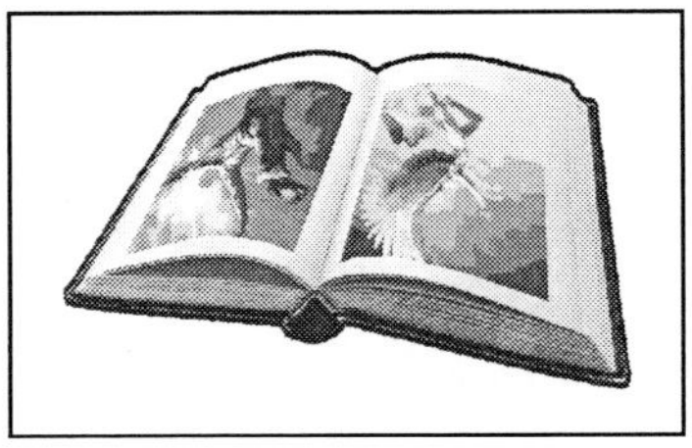

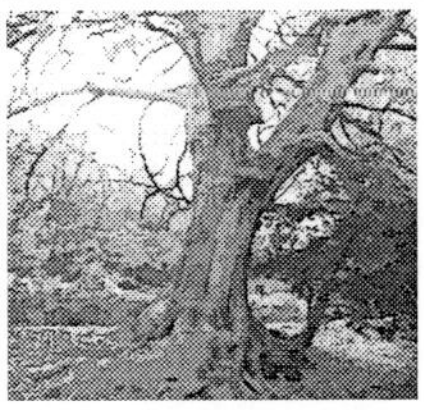

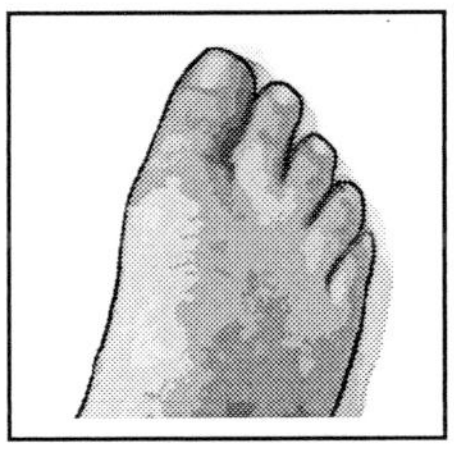

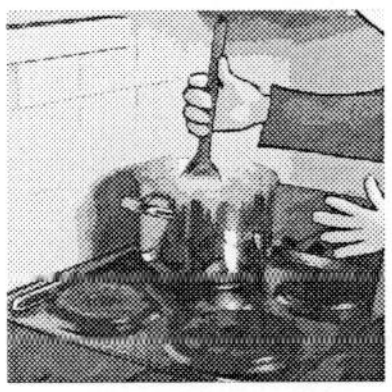

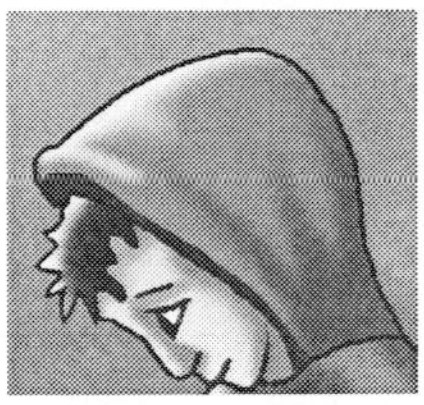

Write the word for each picture. Put one sound in each square.

Level 1 Book 9   'In the Wood'   <oo>

Reading Practice - words with <oo> as in 'book'

book	crook	hood
wood	look	took
brook	shook	foot
good	cook	stood
wool	soot	woof
hook	rook	<oo> as in 'book' words

Level 1 Book 9   'In the Wood'   <oo>

Reading and Comprehension 1 – Make a Book

Dan took Meg to the wood. "Woof!" said Meg. A rabbit ran into the wood. Meg ran into the wood.

Dan ran to look for Meg in the wood. Dan stood still. "Meg! Meg!" he yelled.

"Woof!" said Meg. She was in a trap. Dan took Meg to the vet.

Read the text and draw a picture to match the text on each page. Cut around the boxes and fold into a book.

Level 1 Book 9   'In the Wood'   <oo>

Reading and Comprehension 2 – What's Missing?

Dan took Meg to the vet.   Meg stood on the vet's table. The vet had a good look at Meg's leg. "Traps are not good." He shook his head. "But I can fix Meg's leg."

"Good," said Dan. "Woof!" said Meg.

What's missing in the picture?

Reading Game

Start

Finish

wood	woof	soot	nook	good
took	foot		stood	hood
foot	hood		good	woof
look	rook		brook	soot
stood	wool	shook	look	cook	wood

Play with counters and die. This sheet may be photocopied by the purchaser. © Phonic Books Ltd 2008

4 in a row game <oo> as in 'book'

book	wood	foot	cook	hood
good	wool	took	look	good
shook	rook	stood	wool	cook
brook	foot	nook	soot	book
wood	rook	cook	good	wool
look	hood	book	took	crook
brook	stood	foot	wool	rook

Play with two sets of coloured counters. Two players take turns to read the word and put a counter on the word. Players can make 4 -in-a row horizontally, vertically and diagonally. The winner is the first to get 4 of his/her counters in a row. The winner places a counter on a dandelion. The game is played four times until all the dandelions are covered. This sheet may be photocopied by the purchaser. © Phonic Books Ltd. 2008

The Extended Phonic Code
Level 1 Book 10

'The Fort' - <or>

Page 1 - Word Building and Blending

Page 2 - Segmenting and Spelling
Words: corn, fork, horse, fort, horn

Page 3 - Reading Practice - words with <or>

Page 4 – Reading and Comprehension 1 – Make a Book

Page 5 – Reading Comprehension 2 – What's Missing?

Page 6 - Reading Game

Page 7 – 4-in-a-row Game

Each sheet has it's own instructions.

Level 1 Book 10   'The Fort'   <or>

Word Building and Blending <or>

f		k	
h		se	
c		n	
s	p		t	

| or | or | or | or |

Cut out the <or> squares and slot into the words above. Blend the sounds into a word. Draw
a matching picture of the word in the big box.
This sheet may be photocopied by the purchaser. © Phonics Book Ltd. 2008

Level 1 Book 10   'The Fort'   <or>

Segmenting and Spelling - words with <or>

Level 1 Book 10   'The Fort'   <or>

Reading Practice - words with <or>

fork	lord	fort
corn	worn	short
sport	torn	cord
horn	port	sort
pork	born	storm
stork	snort	<or> words

Level 1 Book 10   'The Fort'   <or>

Reading and Comprehension 1 – Make a Book

Liz makes a fort from
a big box. Dan thinks
it is boring. But then
Wilf gets a bit of elf
dust...

Zap! The box turns
into a big old fort.
Dan is the lord of the
fort. He has a horse.

The kids hop on the
horse.
"Snort, snort!" says
the horse.

Read the text and draw a picture to match the text on each page. Cut around the boxes and fold into a book.
This sheet may be photocopied by the purchaser. © Phonic Books Ltd. 2008

Level 1 Book 10   'The Fort'   <or>

Reading and Comprehension 2 – What's Missing?

Dan and Liz trot on the horse. They pass

the sports club.

"I am the lord of the fort!" says Dan,

"Come and play in my fort."   The kids go

back to play in the fort with Dan and Liz.

What's missing in the picture?

This text follows on from the story 'The Fort'. The pupil reads the text and adds the missing details in the picture below. The pupil can then write his or her own ending to the story.
This sheet may be photocopied by the purchaser. © Phonic Books Ltd. 2008

Start

Finish

fort — stork — sport — port — cord — for — storm

corn — cork — worn — short — born — sport

horse — form — fork — lord — fort

torn — horn — lord — sort — north — horn

4 in a row game <or>

born	fork	acorn	fort	worn
short	cord	port	sort	sport
horn	sort	pork	storm	form
stork	snort	lord	north	horse
worn	for	corn	lord	storm
acorn	north	short	pork	horn
sort	torn	snort	cord	born

Play with two sets of coloured counters. Two players take turns to read the word and put a counter on the word. Players can make 4 -in-a row horizontally, vertically and diagonally. The winner is the first to get 4 of his/her counters in a row. The winner places a counter on a dandelion. The game is played four times until all the dandelions are covered. This sheet may be photocopied by the purchaser. © Phonic Books Ltd. 2008

Reading Game

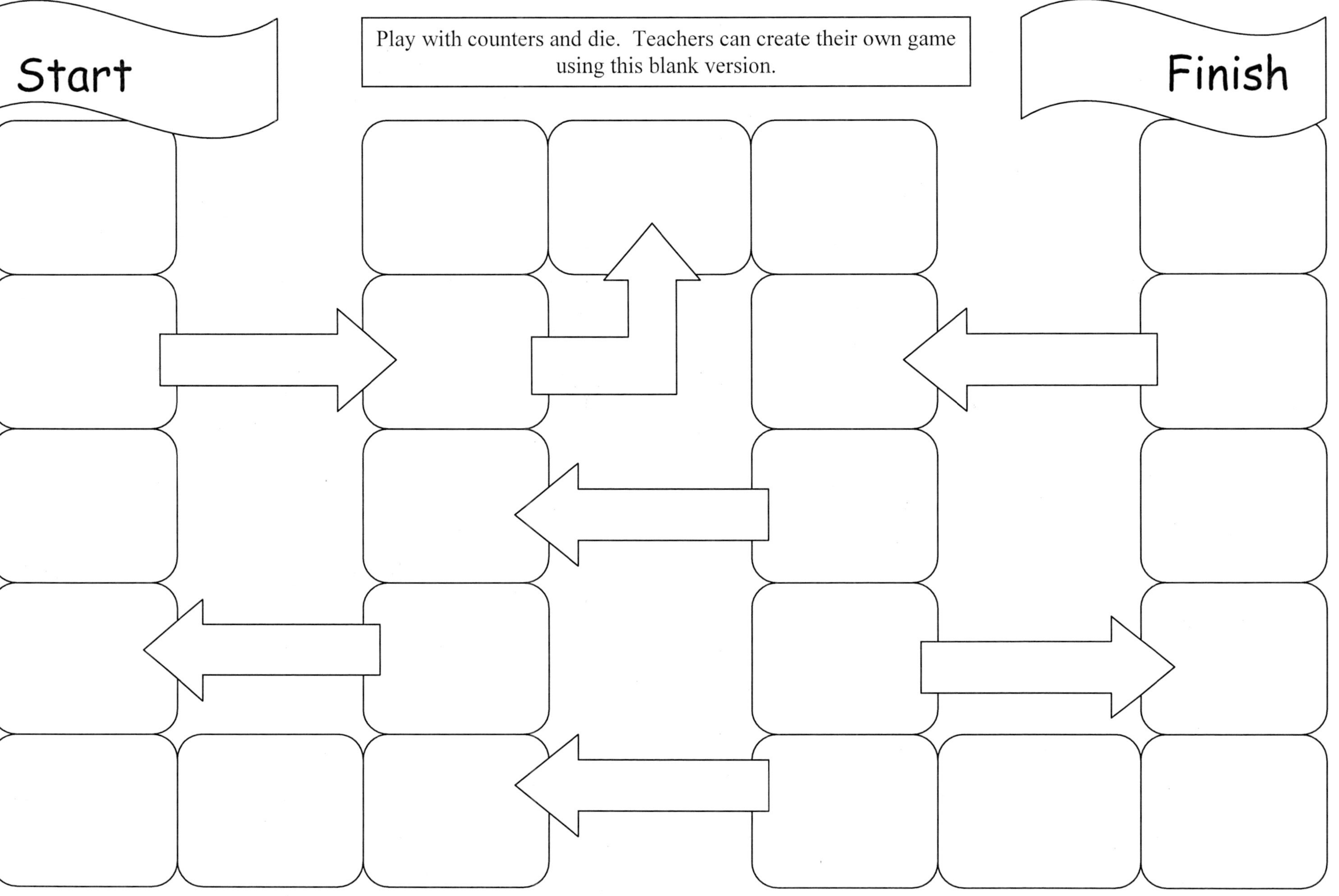

Blank 4 in a row game

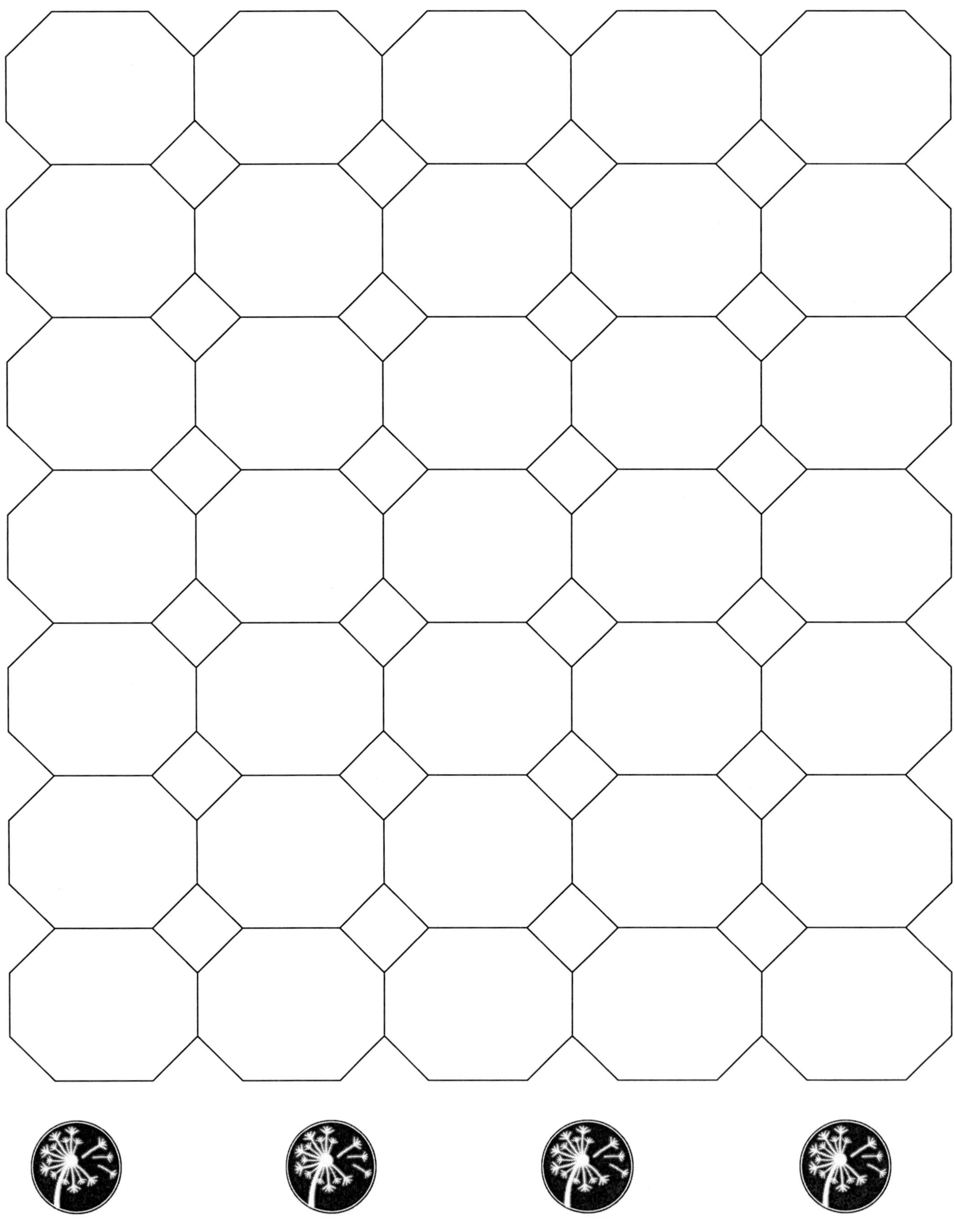